GEOMETRY IN VENICE

MICHAEL MACKENZIE

Playwrights Canada Press
Toronto

Geometry in Venice © Copyright 1990 Michael Mackenzie

Playwrights Canada Press is the publishing imprint of
the Playwrights Union of Canada: 54 Wolseley St., 2nd fl.
Toronto, Ontario CANADA
M5T 1A5
Tel. (416) 947-0201
Fax. (416) 947-0159

Patricia Nye — Christopher Banks & Associates
219 Dufferin St., Ste 305,
Toronto, Ontario CANADA
M6K 1Y9 Tel. (416) 530-4002

Playwrights Canada Press operates with the generous assistance of The
Canada Council - Writing and Publishing Section, and Theatre Section, and
the Ontario Arts Council.

Front cover photo by David Lee.
Edited and designed by Tony Hamill.

Canadian Cataloguing in Publication Data
Michael Mackenzie
      Geometry in venice
A play
ISBN 0-88754-481-9
I. Title.
PS8575.K46G46 1992   C812'.54   C92-094422-1
PR9199.3.M244G46 1992

First edition: September 1992.   Printed and bound in Canada.

For my sisters, Jean and Mary.

Author's Notes

Vitruvius, the Roman writer, tells how a philosopher, shipwrecked on the shores of Rhodes and finding geometrical figures traced in the sand, told his companions that they should not be afraid — here were traces of civilisation. This observation reflects a deeply ingrained belief of Western culture: that learning — the Arts and Sciences — are signs of a deeper humanity. Geometry, in particular, was regarded not just as a sign but as a paradigm in resolving the complexities of human conduct and promoting the fair and ethical treatment of men and women. It's not surprising that such signs could be of paramount importance to the shipwrecked and the helpless.

Most late Victorians would have to look for such signs in the "civilised behaviour" of manners and propriety, and we should not allow differences in period and behavior to disguise a similar quest in our own time. In political and economic upheaval, we, too, grope for signs that even in the most disastrous circumstances there can be mutual understanding that allows us to keep our humanity intact. We cling to the notion that with the complexity of relationships, the disintegration of families and societies, disease, addiction, death, and the loss of love, there is some way of proceeding that is rational, fair and equitable.

Geometry in Venice is set in Venice and Paris in the 1880's, a time, like our own, of prodigious changes. Venice, once a powerhouse of European civilisation, had finally reached its status as a museum city for tourists; a strange, romantic *reductio ad absurdum* of the geometrical impulse embodied in the architecture and perspective painting of the Italian Renaissance. It had also been connected by railway to Paris — the locus of the final subversion of perspecetive-in-painting through Impressionism.

Paris was the city *par excellence* of modernity — mass consumption through department stores and bars, the destruction of the old class ghettoes through urban renewal, the changing economic role of women and the blurring of traditional class distinctions with the final triumph of the cash nexus.

In that mysterious lacuna between cities — neither romantic nor impressionist, classical nor modern — lies the veiled and chimerical eroticism of the paintings of John Singer Sargent. It was Sargent's childhood which inspired the novella, *The Pupil*, by his friend Henry James.

In *Geometry in Venice* we meet the Moreens, a family whose economic viability depends on exploiting the assumptions of a closing epoch, where credit and social access had depended on others' perceptions of class and standing, and appearance could matter more than cash. We also meet a young Canadian, Pemberton, and Henry James.

James wrote about a family, also called Moreen, in *The Pupil*, from the point-perspective of an absent narrator writing in the third person. In the play, he finally gets to meet them. Thus we enter these lives not from the single point of view of a narrator but from the shifting perspective of three people who become intimately involved with each other.

It is their attempts to deal with this intimacy — that mysterious lacuna between people — in disastrous circumstances that presents them with a series of painful dilemmas.

— *M.Mackenzie, 1990*

Geometry in Venice is set in the last decade of the 19th Century in Venice and paris and takes place over a period of months.

The Characters (in order of appearance):

MRS. MOREEN	*An attractive Englishwoman in her late thirties or early forties.*
PEMBERTON	*A young man, Canadian, just out of university in England.*
MORGAN	*A boy, the Moreens' son ,14 or 15 years old. He has a hole in his heart.*
MOREEN	*An Englishman in his late forties.*
AMY	*A young woman of 23, the Moreens' daughter.*
JAMES	*An independently-wealthy American author.*

Geometry in Venice was first performed by Theatre Plus Toronto, St. Lawrence Centre, Toronto, April 5th 1990, with the following cast:

MRS. MOREEN	*Barbara Gordon*
PEMBERTON	*Tom McCamus*
MORGAN	*Matthew Ferguson*
MOREEN	*Craig Davidson*
AMY	*Chick Reid*
JAMES	*Richard Binsley*

Directed by Peter Hinton.
Designed by Michael Levine.
Costumes by John Ferguson.
Lighting by Kevin Lamotte.
Stage manager - Susan Konynenburg.

Acknowledgements

Special thanks are due to Robin Phillips for his encouragement and discussion of the early drafts.

For the production at Theatre Plus Toronto, my deepest gratitude to all the cast for their enthusiasm and commitment, to John Ferguson — particularily for his immaculate rendering of the dresses from Sargent's paintings, to Michael Levine for his wonderful, evocative set. Thanks and admiration to Duncan McIntosh for betting on a dark horse to open his first season as Artistic Director.

And, of course, deepest appreciation for the energy and dedication of Peter Hinton in giving the play an exquisite production.

— *Michael Mackenzie*

Act One, Scene One

Lights up slowly in a rather splendid apartment in Venice, MORGAN *is at stage left looking out over the audience as if from a balcony.* MRS. MOREEN *enters followed by* PEMBERTON.

MRS. MOREEN   I think that's everything. (*pause*) The room, as you see is comfortable with good light and cool, cool for Venice.

PEMBERTON   It does sound as if we might suit quite well.

MRS. MOREEN   I think you could be quite content. Content but stimulated. Even for a graduate of Oxford. Morgan is a very stimulating young man.

PEMBERTON   (*quietly*) Er, Cambridge actually...

MRS. MOREEN   And you may take your meals with us or you may prefer to eat out, away from the *melée* as it were. (*laughing*)

Silence.

PEMBERTON   As Venice is an expensive city I shall mostly be eating with you, depending...

MRS. MOREEN (*overlapping*) Quite recent too, the American tourists. Nice on the other hand — quite reasonable. And Rome, even Rome compared with Venice...even London. But London, such a Philistine city I find. Mr. Moreen is there at the moment, on business. (*pause*) You know London Mr. Pemberton?

PEMBERTON While I was at university I took advantage of a small inheritance, which — while it lasted — I used to explore London, and Paris.

MRS. MOREEN Oh Mr. Pemberton...a young man in Paris — (*finger-wagging*) eh, eh, eh.

PEMBERTON Which is why, now, I have to search for gainful employment...

MORGAN 'Eh, eh, eh', *mere?*

PEMBERTON ...which I am quite happy to do, given — of course — that we can reach a suitable arrangement.

Pause.

MRS. MOREEN Morgan dear. I seem to have left my fan *quelque part*, would you like to look for it?

MORGAN *rises.* MRS. MOREEN *watches him go.*

MRS. MOREEN Close the door, *liebchen*

MORGAN Drafts *mater?*

MRS. MOREEN *Esattamente, carissimo*

MORGAN *exits.*

MRS. MOREEN   Now Mr. Pemberton, Morgan is quite an exceptional little man. He has come on wonderfully in the bosom of the family, but now he is of an age. Which is why Mr. Moreen and I wish to place our confidence in a university man. And you are a university man.

PEMBERTON   Oh yes.

MRS. MOREEN   Is that unusual for a Canadian?

PEMBERTON   I don't think so.

MRS. MOREEN   My husband wants a classical education. Also the sciences. You do have the sciences Mr. Pemberton?

PEMBERTON   Yes. But I'm surprised that, at his age, you're not sending Morgan to one of the better schools, in England.

MRS. MOREEN   We would have. But all such reflection...All is overclouded by this (*touching her left breast*) a weakness, a flaw. He cannot play, Mr. Pemberton, he cannot play as other children do.

PEMBERTON   (*pause*) I'm sorry..?

MRS. MOREEN   His heart.

MORGAN enters.

MORGAN   I couldn't find it.

MRS. MOREEN   *Ça ne fait rien, carissima.* (*pause, rising*) Well, Mr. Pemberton, that seems to be everything. I really shouldn't take up your time any longer.

PEMBERTON rises.

PEMBERTON   I was wondering...

MRS. MOREEN   Yes?

PEMBERTON   What exactly — well not exactly — what you, or Mr. Moreen, would have in mind in terms of remuneration...payment.

MRS. MOREEN   I can assure you that all that will be quite regular. As soon as he comes back from London you shall have it out with Mr. Moreen.

PEMBERTON   Oh, I don't imagine we shall have much of a battle.

MORGAN   Ask for anything you like. We're so agreeable.

MRS. MOREEN   Morgan dear. (*to* PEMBERTON) You can see what to expect.

MORGAN   And the less you expect the better. But we are not dull, certainly not that.

MRS. MOREEN   And we owe it all to you. (*to* PEMBERTON) Well then, on Friday.

                   PEMBERTON *goes to speak.*

MRS. MOREEN   Mind you don't fail us.

MORGAN   (*directly to* PEMBERTON) Do you *want* to come?

PEMBERTON   (*brief hesitation*) It's hard to see how I could refuse.

MORGAN   Well, I'll do the best I can for you.

> MORGAN *walks out to the balcony.*
> *Pause.*

MRS. MOREEN   Thank you Mr. Pemberton. Till Friday then?

> MRS. MOREEN *puts out a hand.*
> PEMBERTON *doesn't know whether to*
> *kiss it or shake it. He shakes it.*

PEMBERTON   Till Friday. (*looking after* MORGAN)

MRS. MOREEN   Leave him. He is...of an age. Much the most interesting person here. But we're all good you know!

PEMBERTON   I'm sure.

MRS. MOREEN   We think he's ready for a tutor.

***

Act One, Scene Two

The same apartment one week later.
MOREEN *and* PEMBERTON *are
talking.* MRS. MOREEN *and* AMY *are
there.*

MOREEN But I feel bound to say that Mr. Pemberton, first-rate chap that you obviously are, you're a little lacking in—shall we say—*style* when it comes down to dealing. Not much of a horse trader.

PEMBERTON I'm sorry?

MOREEN (*to* MRS. MOREEN) You see what I mean? (*to* PEMBERTON) You see what I mean? Got to speak out man to man, no shilly-shallying. University man are you?

MRS. MOREEN Cambridge, dear.

MOREEN (*to* PEMBERTON) Cambridge..?

PEMBERTON I'm sor...what? Yes.

MOREEN Good, good. Glad to see Mrs. Moreen has been looking out for us in my absence.

MRS. MOREEN What's that dear?

MOREEN	Just saying good choice my dear, excellent choice.
MRS. MOREEN	(*beaming briefly at* PEMBERTON) I thought so.
PEMBERTON	Thank you.
MOREEN	No, no, my dear fellow. Take it as your due. Stand up, look the world in the eye and let it know what you're worth, eh? Now you're going to be a tutor to my son Morgan. So, Mr. Pemberton, no beating about the bush — what are you worth?
MRS. MOREEN	What's that dear?
MOREEN	We're having it out my dear.
MRS. MOREEN	Oh, good! Doing battle...
MOREEN	Doing battle!? Are we doing battle Mr. Pemberton?
PEMBERTON	I hardly think...
MRS. MOREEN	He didn't think there'd be much of one, did you Mr. Pemberton.
PEMBERTON	Well —
MOREEN	No, no, no. By all means, we must do battle. A man of the world, Mr. Pemberton, is always prepared to sally forth to do battle. Isn't that so my dear?
MRS. MOREEN	My husband is a man of the world Mr. Pemberton. You just sallied forth to London, didn't you dear?

MOREEN I did indeed. And do you know why I sallied forth to London, Mr. Pemberton?

PEMBERTON No, I'm afraid I don't. To do battle perhaps?

MOREEN (*laughing heartily*) Excellent. (*to* MRS. MOREEN) Exceptional choice, my dear.

MRS. MOREEN Thank you. (*pause*) What *was* it you sallied forth for, again, dear? I forget.

MOREEN To look out, my dear.

MRS. MOREEN (*reminded*) Ah, yes.

MOREEN That is why I go to London, Mr. Pemberton. To look out. You will appreciate, as a university man, that this vigilance is not simply my occupation, but it is our theory of life. We all look out, and we are quite frank about the necessity of doing so. We are earnest people. To a cursory glance our gaiety, our *joie de vivre*, could be perceived as flippancy. Nothing could be further from the truth. We are earnest people, and though we have our fortune — quite adequate I should add for the needs of earnest people — it requires careful and considered administration. Amelia, my daughter, does up her hair and her frocks herself. My wife is able, under the circumstances of my temporary absence, to make capable decisions, as in your own case Pemberton. And I am glad that I can put aside my own needs in favour of the interest inspired by the character and culture of our son Morgan. His education must naturally be of the best — we are counting on you Pemberton — within the limits of our modest means. And I'm am sure my wife will join with me in welcoming you to our

MOREEN   (*continued*) efforts in that regard. (*resting his hand* MRS. MOREEN *as they look at* PEMBERTON)

MRS. MOREEN   I will indeed my dear. I will indeed.

Pause.

PEMBERTON   Thank you.

***

Act One, Scene Three

The next day. MORGAN *and* PEMBERTON.

PEMBERTON   I suppose I should ask first of all if you have any books.

MORGAN   Not so many. (*handing a few books. one by one to* PEMBERTON). We don't keep books. I think mother has a few special ones. These are the ones we've bought since we arrived in Venice.

PEMBERTON   (*looking at the books*) You move around a lot?

MORGAN   Oh, yes. We've been to all kinds of interesting cities, it's exciting.

PEMBERTON   Then that should stand you in good stead for geography. You've got a copy of Caesar's *Gallic Wars*. That's good.

MORGAN   I thought it was rather dull actually. He really fancies himself, and likes to talk about all these different ways of killing people.

PEMBERTON   I see. So you've read it then?

MORGAN   Sort of.

PEMBERTON   "Sort of"'. You read some Latin?

MORGAN   Well, in Italy it's easier to get Latin books than English ones. Most of them are boring religious stuff. My favorite was *De Strategem.* Full of helpful hints like how to float elephants across rivers and things.

PEMBERTON   *De Strategem...?*

MORGAN   By Frontinus Sextus. He wrote that thing about the plumbing too, you know...

PEMBERTON   (*thinking*) *De Aquis Urbana...*

MORGAN   That's it. How to get the bath water for a lot of Romans. He mentions another chap who sounds like he might be sort of interesting...Vitru something.

PEMBERTON   (*still thinking*) Vitruvius — *De Architectura...*

MORGAN   That's it —

PEMBERTON   You seem to be quite accomplished in the Latin language then.

MORGAN   Perhaps we could get that — Vitruvius. I like going to the book shops.

PEMBERTON   You like going to book shops. So you know all your conjugations and declensions?

MORGAN   My what?

PEMBERTON   Conjugations...*amo, amas, amat...amamus, amatis, amant.*

MORGAN   *Amo...amas...amat...?*

PEMBERTON	*Amo* — I love, *amas* — you love, *amat* — he, she, or it loves.
MORGAN	Yes?
PEMBERTON	What?
MORGAN	What do we love?
PEMBERTON	Anything.
MORGAN	Anything?!
PEMBERTON	Well, anything we want to love.
MORGAN	That's an interesting idea.
PEMBERTON	I mean...(*thinking*) It's a way of demonstrating all the forms of the verb *amo*. It changes its form depending on who's doing the loving. And the pronoun — I or you — is contained in the verb so instead of two words you have one. I love...*amo*. The suffix 'o' stands for I. You love...*amas*. He, she or it loves...*amat*.
MORGAN	(*pause*) Yes?
PEMBERTON	Well It's a way of practicing, of learning, the correct form of the verb to use under any specific circumstances.
MORGAN	What specific circumstances?
PEMBERTON	What?
MORGAN	What circumstances had you in mind?

PEMBERTON	Well, any circumstances at all. That's the point. You learn the form — the rules — of the language so you can apply it...them. It's grammar. Haven't you done any grammar at all?
MORGAN	My mother says I'm very good at languages. I help her with translating things.
PEMBERTON	Translating things?
MORGAN	Books and things.
PEMBERTON	But you haven't done any grammar...I think the first book we'll buy will be a Latin grammar. Then we can give *Gallic Wars* a thorough going over.
MORGAN	D'you think that'll help?
PEMBERTON	Help what?
MORGAN	Help anything?
PEMBERTON	It's the best way to learn Latin.
MORGAN	Can't we just speak it?
PEMBERTON	It's not, essentially, a spoken language. It's a written language, as in...(*indicating book*) the *Gallic Wars.*
MORGAN	Oh. (*pause*) I've mostly spoken it.
PEMBERTON	Spoken it? Who to?
MORGAN	There's lots of clerics in Italy — priests and people. They like to talk in Latin.
PEMBERTON	You talk to priests in Latin?

MORGAN	You meet them all the time as you walk around. They always seem to have some piece of gothic architecture they want to show you...pointing out little stone cherubs as they gambol around the eaves.
PEMBERTON	And you speak Latin with them?
MORGAN	The cherubs..?
PEMBERTON	The priests.
MORGAN	Don't you think it important to do battle with the forces of superstition at an early age?
PEMBERTON	It's also important, at an early age, to learn to speak correctly, grammatically.
MORGAN	(*pause*) Is that different to the way we're speaking now?
PEMBERTON	Well, no. That is the way that we're speaking now.
MORGAN	Why don't we speak Latin like this then?
PEMBERTON	We are native English speakers. That's why we can speak English spontaneously...just like that.
MORGAN	Can't we do that with Latin too...just like that?
PEMBERTON	But we have to learn it first, to speak it correctly. And that requires grammar — that's the discipline of learning.
MORGAN	Oh, discipline. That's not a particularly strong point with the Moreens. And the priests always tell me I speak very well — *puer qui linguam angelorum emendate dixit*...then they show me

MORGAN   (*continued*) the cherubs (*pause*) though I never
                 quite saw the connection. *Ego puero repuerasceo.*

PEMBERTON   *Repuerasceo..?!*

MORGAN   It means to be like a boy again. They do that
                 sometimes — stick words together like Germans.

                         Pause.

PEMBERTON   Have you done any mathematics?

                         ***

Act One, Scene Four

> *The same room, morning, the sun is streaming in.* MOREEN *is shaving, collarless.* MORGAN *is sitting engrossed in a book.* PEMBERTON *enters.*

PEMBERTON   I'm sorry.

MOREEN   Ah. Pemberton.

> MRS. MOREEN *enters.*

MRS. MOREEN   Shaving..?

MOREEN   Shaving.

MRS. MOREEN   ...In the drawing room..?!

MORGAN   (*not looking up*) Father's shaving, I'm reading, and Mr. Pemberton is sorry. That brings us up to date — in the drawing room at least.

MRS. MOREEN   Thank you dear.

MOREEN   And what, my dear Pemberton, could you be sorry for on such an ideal day.

MRS. MOREEN   I'm not sure that *I'm* not sorry, dearest...That
              which might have been an ideal day is somewhat
              marred.

MOREEN   Let's not be fastidious, my dear. I think it best to
              surrender ourselves to this wonderful day as we
              find it. Eh Pemberton?

PEMBERTON   Er...I'd have to think about it.

MRS. MOREEN   Exactly! — to be thoughtful. A man prepared for
              the ideal day, so he will not be caught,
              metaphorically speaking, shaving in the drawing
              room.

MOREEN   Could it not be though, that shaving in the
              drawing room is part of the ideal day?
              Pemberton?

PEMBERTON   I imagine that's a possibility.

MRS. MOREEN   Not for me.

MOREEN   What?

MRS. MOREEN   Shaving in the drawing room is not a possibility
              for me.

MOREEN   Ah! Some equivalent perhaps? No I suppose not.

              Pause.

PEMBERTON   Then we do have a sort of philosophical
              objection. According to Plato, the ideal must be
              universal. And shaving in the drawing room, as
              Mrs. Moreen pointed out is not — nor can be —
              universal.

MOREEN	Excellent. I imagine Plato shaved in the drawing room. I'm sure they had drawing rooms. After all they were a civilised people, the Greeks, eh, Pemberton?
MRS. MOREEN	But I seem to recall Plato thought men more 'universal' than women.
MOREEN	Exactly the point I would have made, my dear. Which only shows what profound thoughts can strike one while shaving in the drawing room. (*pause*) Plato probably had all his good ideas shaving in the drawing room.
MRS. MOREEN	You're a Platonist, Mr. Pemberton?
PEMBERTON	I think he's important for a classical education.
MOREEN	And I understand that he is particularly favoured at Cambridge.
MRS. MOREEN	I sometimes have my doubts that a classical education, whatever its favourites, is a good thing.
	AMY *enters, not dressed but decent.* PEMBERTON *tries to conceal his embarrassment.*
AMY	So this is where everybody is. (*sitting down, to* MORGAN) So what are we up to today?
MORGAN	(*still reading*) Mother's getting Platonic with Mr. Pemberton.
AMY	If that's all I think I'll go back to bed.

MRS. MOREEN   No Amy dear, the Dorringtons are having a day today, we should be there. And you should get dressed dear. We don't want to traumatise Mr. Pemberton with our over-familiar domesticity.

AMY   But father's shaving. In the drawing room.

Silence.

MRS. MOREEN   Amelia...dressed, dear, please. You must be gracious but arresting for your admirers at the Dorrington's.

AMY   Shouldn't we try something a little different? Weren't we gracious but arresting at the FitzWarren's last Wednesday.

MOREEN   But if you are not gracious but arresting, Amy, what are you to be? We have always been gracious but arresting.

MRS. MOREEN   You have a point, Amy dear. Perhaps a little variation is in order. With our extensive social commitments we must not be dull. It is not something we can afford.

> *Finished his shaving,* MOREEN *rises and exits.*

MORGAN   (*putting book aside*) Well, you could try...elegant but congenial?

AMY   Couldn't it be something a little more...aloof...imposing?

MORGAN   Distinctively arresting but elegantly congenial?

MRS. MOREEN   Couldn't we have something a touch more *outré*?

Pause.

MORGAN   Elegantly distinctive but arrestingly congenial..?

AMY   I'm not sure that's quite it.

MORGAN   Distinctively elegant yet congenitally arrested..?

MRS. MOREEN   Hardly a formula for conspicuous nubility, Morgan dear.

PEMBERTON   Nubility..? Is that a word?

MRS. MOREEN   Of course it's a word...In at least three languages.

AMY   Congenitally arrested seems to fit any number of the nubile men I find myself with.

MRS. MOREEN   Men are not nubile, Amy dear. Girls are nubile. Men are wealthy.

AMY   Johannus is a Prince.

MRS. MOREEN   Then I'm sure he will find a suitable match.

> MOREEN *enters with some mail, holds a letter up.*

AMY   Is that for me?

MOREEN   No. This is not a prostrate suitor. It has about it a cold and institutional air.

AMY   Johannus is prostrate.

MOREEN   In every sense of the word. Johannus is hardly fertile ground for financial expectations. The family is completely broke. He should find a young lady in a position to exchange her money

MOREEN	(*continued*) for a title. I think Americans like to do that sort of thing. (*reading the envelope with pince-nez*) Oh? (*to* MRS. MOREEN) It's for you my dear.
MRS. MOREEN	For me?
MOREEN	(*looking*) It's from your publisher.
MRS. MOREEN	(*brightening*) Am I dressed to receive a letter from my publisher?
PEMBERTON	I didn't realise you were an author.
MRS. MOREEN	An author..?
PEMBERTON	A novelist? A poet?
MRS. MOREEN	A novelist? God Forbid. And I leave the poetry to young men who can afford waistcoats in appropriately bad taste.
MOREEN	My wife is a translator, Pemberton. A translator of 'precision yet refinement'...wasn't that what the chap in *The Times* said?
MRS. MOREEN	(*looking at the envelope*) What he meant was that I was able to render all those rude Italian words innocuous to the Anglican sensibility.
AMY	What rude Italian words were they mother?
MOREEN	Amy dear. In front of Mr. Pemberton...and your young brother.
MORGAN	(*still reading*) It's alright. I already know all those rude Italian words. I even rendered some of them innocuous.

MRS. MOREEN   (*to* PEMBERTON) Morgan was a goldmine of synonym and euphemism in my struggle with the muse. And he was only...twelve?..at the time. (*opening the letter*) Let's see what appreciation there is of 'precision and refinement'.

> *Everyone, except* PEMBERTON *and* MORGAN, *are suddenly paying close attention. Pause.* MRS. MOREEN *reads.*

MRS. MOREEN   Well. My publisher has enclosed a flattering review from a very reputable literary journal...

MOREEN   Very nice my dear...

MRS. MOREEN   And a less than flattering bank draft for royalties...(*handing a check to her husband*).

> MOREEN *looks at the check, disappointed. Pause.*

AMY   Shouldn't Maria be bringing the breakfast?

MRS. MOREEN   It's Maria's day off.

AMY   I thought we gave her the weekends off?

MOREEN   And Wednesdays. There is so little for her to do.

AMY   I'm hungry.

MRS. MOREEN   They'll be plenty to eat at the Dorrington's. Enough for a nubile young lady.

MORGAN   What about my tutor and me?

MRS. MOREEN   (*rising*) Amy and I will make some breakfast for you and your tutor.

Act One, Scene Five

> PEMBERTON *and* MORGAN *at work.*
> PEMBERTON *is marking.*

PEMBERTON I liked your essay Morgan. You've obviously learned a lot about Venice while you've been here. Take a look at the spelling. (*giving some paper to* MORGAN) So how are you getting on with that Greek grammar?

MORGAN Oh, fine. Funny way to learn a language though. To start with anyway, but then you realise it's pretty good — if you're not going to speak it, it's a good way to learn.

PEMBERTON You're not having any difficulty with it?

MORGAN Not really. Some of the grammar words — like gerund — stump you at first. But then you get the hang of it.

PEMBERTON You've got that far?

MORGAN What?

PEMBERTON Reading about gerunds.

MORGAN Oh, yes.

PEMBERTON	So how far did you get?
MORGAN	I finished it.
PEMBERTON	You what?
MORGAN	I finished it. Shouldn't I have?
PEMBERTON	When did you read it?
MORGAN	Yesterday, and this morning.
PEMBERTON	This morning? In the drawing room?
MORGAN	But I think I'll have to read it again.
PEMBERTON	Really.
MORGAN	You know. To remember it all.
PEMBERTON	Perhaps we could do some of the excercises at the back of the book. That's often the best way to memorize.
MORGAN	(*pulling a folded, creased piece of paper out of his pocket*) Oh, I did some of those.
PEMBERTON	You did?
MORGAN	It looked like sort of fun.
	Pause while PEMBERTON *spreads and looks at the paper.*
PEMBERTON	This is...where did you get the vocabulary?
MORGAN	At the end of the book. But, you know, after you taught me the Greek alphabet it's kind of obvious what a lot of the words are. Once you know the

MORGAN	(*continued*) letters you can see how they're like some Latin or English words.
PEMBERTON	(*still reading*) This is quite good.
MORGAN	It's fun as a language. Not many words but you can do lots with them.
PEMBERTON	Fun. Well, your Greek is coming along Morgan. Perhaps we should get onto the sciences right away. Some mathematics.
MORGAN	Mathematics sounds so...unstylish.
PEMBERTON	You think so? Most people are impressed by the idea of science. They don't know much about it but they're inpressed. (*producing a book and handing it to* MORGAN) Here. I found a copy of Euclid's *Elements of Geometry*.
MORGAN	(*taking it*) You got this? (*opening it*) Who was Euclid?
PEMBERTON	He was a Greek, lived in Alexandria. I really think you'll enjoy geometry. You seem to have the perfect brain for languages but it's different to learning a language. It'll be a challenge.
MORGAN	How so?
PEMBERTON	Well...It's a system. A perfectly rigorous, enclosed self-sufficient system not like a language at all. Think of all those cities you've seen. A language is like some sort of sprawling city, its old city center — its origins...then the well-planned environs of the city administration, its dictionary and its rules of grammar...then the suburbs — like the sciences, physics — full of new elegances and ambitions...the slums, full of

PEMBERTON (*continued*) profanities, where most of us only dare go when we're drunk and a little bloody-minded. I thought I could teach you Latin by making you learn the official city map, then I find that you've already thoroughly explored the city — what's left of it — and learned it perfectly well, without a map. But geometry is not like that. It's not like a city...arbitrary, ambiguous, sometimes confusing like a language. It's a system...*the* system...of flat — two-dimensional — space. It's not about any particular space, but the very possibility of space...extension, latitude, longitude — the very possibility of all those things that speak of form, shape, dimension...architecture, navigation, geography, cartograghy, astronomy...they're all based on geometry. It has five axioms, five propositions which are obviously and self-evidently true.

MORGAN Like what?

PEMBERTON Like...the shortest distance between two points is a straight line.

MORGAN Well that's pretty obvious.

PEMBERTON Exactly. But from those five propositions one can construct, step by step, a perfect, inevitable edifice, that can describe all the possible shapes in space.

MORGAN But the things you construct, aren't they obvious?

PEMBERTON Well...yes, but not straight away. That's what makes it so...extraordinary. It's not invented, the way people invent a language, it's discovered. A French mathematician — Blaise Pascal — when he was a boy, worked out a number of Euclid's

PEMBERTON   (*continued*) proofs, entirely on his own, in his room, without ever having been told anything about geometry. You find your way through languages so well. But languages change and they're not necessarily clear — like the city with all its twists and turns — there's often so much hidden or ambiguous...confusing. But with mathematics you'll have the chance to think something through, step by step. And once you have it, it's perfectly clear, for ever. It's completely sure and secure, it never changes.

MORGAN   I don't see how that could work.

PEMBERTON   We are going to need a blackboard and chalk. I think it's going to be good for you to do something unstylish.

MORGAN   A blcakboard? did the Greeks use blackboards?

PEMBERTON   I'm sure they didn't.

MORGAN   So how did they do geometry.

PEMBERTON   (*thinking*) They used to trace their fingers in the sand.

MORGAN   Perhaps you and I could go to Greece then to do our geometry...for the sand, you know.

PEMBERTON   I don't think we could quite afford that.

MORGAN   Can we afford a blackboard and chalk?

PEMBERTON   (*slightly defensive*) I have some money with me.

MORGAN   At any rate then, you'll hang on to the last.

PEMBERTON   Hang on..?

MORGAN   Till the Moreens have finished you off.

MORGAN *and* PEMBERTON *exit.*

***

Act One, Scene Six

> MOREEN *enters on* PEMBERTON
> *alone in the drawing room.*

MOREEN Ah, Pemberton! How goes it? How is our little Da Vinci? I hear that you are on the sciences now. The sciences have become essential, this was an observation I made to my wife just the other day; the sciences have become essential, I said. And the family could never have hoped to broaden young Morgan the way you are doing. (*pause, softer*) Nice lad isn't he. I do so...admire him. Courageous. But for a flaw he might have been...anything. Statesman, explorer...

> MRS. MOREEN *enters with tea things.*

MOREEN Wasn't I saying, dear, they are essential now, the sciences. Didn't I observe that just the other day?

MRS. MOREEN (*organising tea things*) I think you did dear. Is Morgan lying down, Mr. Pemberton?

PEMBERTON No. I left him with a problem.

MOREEN A scientific problem I trust, Pemberton?

PEMBERTON A geometrical problem.

MOREEN	Good, good. The sciences you know (*groping*) electricity...chemistry...biology — flora and fauna. You have a great deal in Canada, more even than the Americans I understand..
PEMBERTON	Sciences..?
MOREEN	Flora and fauna. (*brief pause*) And it is reassuring to know that we can count on you Pemberton.
PEMBERTON	I...was wondering if we might discuss for a moment my employment as Morgan's tutor.
MOREEN	Absolutely! No, no, no, Pemberton. Never doubt our readiness to look out for our son's education. That is what we do, look out...whatever the vista may be.
PEMBERTON	That is very reassuring.
MOREEN	My dear, should you have sunf that song at the Dittwhistles's? A little risque perhaps
MRS. MOREEN	They couldn't understand the words. Neopolitani is somewhat beyond the grasp of Americans — the Episcopalian temperment, I believe. But they were entertained, I think. (*singing some more*) Carnival, Mr. Pemberton. Carnival.
PEMBERTON	Yes, I —
MRS. MOREEN	What *is* Morgan's problem?
PEMBERTON	(*off guard*) What?
MRS. MOREEN	The geometrical problem that you left with him.
PEMBERTON	Er...it's proof for Pythagoras' theorum. I left him looking for a proof for Pythagoras.

MRS. MOREEN   Is that difficult?

PEMBERTON   It's not elementry.

MRS. MOREEN   I hope he won't be vexed by geometry, Mr. Pemberton. A gifted boy...but his heart, the slightest strain.

MOREEN   You must watch him closely to see he does not become vexed.

PEMBERTON   When I left him he was quite at ease.

MRS. MOREEN   But you do understand our concern.

PEMBERTON   You've mentioned Morgan's condition. (*pause*) I was hoping we might discuss my employment...as Morgan's tutor.

MOREEN   As you said my dear fellow...and let me reiterate my readiness to engage the topic — no hesitancy or false delicacy is necessary. I am a man of the world, Pemberton, and let me exhort you to be one too. Morgan is, as we know maturing, he is...(*meaningfully*) of an age.

PEMBERTON   I don't quite understand.

MOREEN   I should tell you that the doctors have warned us. Puberty will be a great strain on his heart, eh, my dear? The sad burden of Morgan's approaching youth. (*to* PEMBERTON) Tragic that the rising sap, the blossoming forth to manhood, may prove the fatal hurdle...

MRS. MOREEN   That is why we are so grateful for your interest, Mr. Pemberton...watching over Morgan.

PEMBERTON	I actually hoped to be able to discuss my renumeration. As Morgan's tutor.
MOREEN	Of course, of course. What can I do for you? Be forthright, Pemberton, as I have said I am a man of the world, with me it must be plain dealing.
PEMBERTON	Well, I'm not sure I can continue without a little money.
MOREEN	Pemberton! I didn't realise my dear fellow. How long have you been with us now?
PEMBERTON	Almost a month.
MOREEN	Almost a month! And what funds have you received?
PEMBERTON	Only ten francs, so far. I mentioned earlier that I arrived in your employ with a number of small debts which I hoped to clear.
MOREEN	Of course, of course. Only ten francs? I must confess myself a little shocked. (*to* MRS. MOREEN) Aren't you a little shocked my dear? We must go into this at the first possible opportunity, the first possible opportunity...
MRS. MOREEN	(*to* MOREEN) We are expecting a guest at any moment dear.
MOREEN	A guest, my dear?
MRS. MOREEN	A Mr. James is escorting Amelia home.
MOREEN	Mr. James?
MRS. MOREEN	A writer.

MOREEN   A writer? Hardly a respectable enterprise in a
                       man.

MRS. MOREEN   (*to* MOREEN) The James' are one of the
                       inordinately wealthy pillars of the New York
                       establishment. And our Mr. James is intimately
                       connected.

MOREEN   Ah. New York,eh? Quite a thriving little place.

MRS. MOREEN   And he is quite entertaining.

MOREEN   Excellent. Well, Pemberton. We will take all the
                       necessary steps to solve the problem, be assured
                       the problem will be solved.

PEMBERTON   (*rising*) I wonder if I might have some indication
                       of an arrangement. It has been rather difficult, if
                       not impossible, to see you and your wife alone
                       — away from Amy and Morgan. And this is not
                       a topic I feel we should discuss in front of them.

MRS. MOREEN   You wouldn't mention this to Morgan then? He
                       doesn't know?

PEMBERTON   No, no.

MOREEN   We appreciate your delicacy, Pemberton. It
                       shows style. (*rising*) Excuse me, but I must look
                       into this immediately, mustn't I dear?
                       Immediately.

                                   MOREEN *exits.* MRS. MOREEN *is
                                   deep in thought.* PEMBERTON *is lost
                                   for words. Pause.*

MRS. MOREEN (*still thinking*) I must admit though that I think that we've all been getting on splendidly, splendidly!

PEMBERTON I'm very afraid that unless I can receive some funds very soon I might have to leave.

MRS. MOREEN But that would be dreadful...

PEMBERTON I have a number of debts that I must clear..

MRS. MOREEN But leave us, and Morgan..? (*pause, studying* PEMBERTON) You won't. You know you won't — you're too interested. You *are* interested, you know you are, you dear kind man!

> *Sounds - off,* AMY's *voice.* AMY *enters followed by* JAMES. PEMBERTON *rises.* AMY *is laughing as if at a slightly risqué joke. She is obviously enamoured of* JAMES.

MRS. MOREEN Mr. James! So kind of you to walk Amy home. I hope she was sufficiently stimulating company..?

JAMES Indeed. Let me congratulate you on a remarkable daughter. A very literate young lady.

> MRS. MOREEN *nods acknowledgement. Slight pause.*

MRS. MOREEN Let me introduce Mr. Pemberton. Mr. Pemberton is our son, Morgan's, tutor.

> JAMES *and* PEMBERTON *exchanging slight bows.*

JAMES	(*to* MRS. MOREEN) The remarkable Morgan you spoke of. (*to* PEMBERTON) It must be quite a challenge to coach such a little prodigy.
PEMBERTON	It has its hurdles, (*including* MRS. MOREEN) but I trust they can be overcome.
MRS. MOREEN	(*to* PEMBERTON) Mr. James was the novelist of the party.
JAMES	Not the only one —
AMY	He was telling me that Mrs. Stormer is a writer too.
MRS. MOREEN	Mrs. Stormer. Really..?
AMY	Mrs. Stormer is Greville Fane!
JAMES	She is widely read amoung Americans, and often receives invitations to their 'days'.
AMY	Mr. James said that, as she writes about aristocratic passions but talks about the price of bottled water, she is usually a disappointment.
MRS. MOREEN	(*mock scold*) Mr. James...
JAMES	Her son too, I understand is an aspiring writer. She tells me that she is tutoring him as a novelist.
MRS. MOREEN	Her son...?
AMY	He was the magnificently fat young man with the red face. Leolin Stormer.

MRS. MOREEN Oh him! I've seen him at a number of functions. His principal attribute seems to be an extensive wardrobe.

AMY ...An extraordinarily *outré* way of dressing...

MRS. MOREEN He once confided in me that 'there was no manual so important to him as the massive book of life'. Though it was unclear to me where a man of his talents and breeding got the funds to peruse such an expensive volume.

JAMES But now you see. Greville Fane has been a prodigious author.

MRS. MOREEN Indeed. She must support the family quite well.

JAMES As much as three novels a year.

AMY Mr. James said she is so tireless because she only writes from the elbow down.

JAMES And I understand she gets a great deal for her novels. I must admit the revelation gave me quite a pang — not of envy you understand but from the recognition that, practicing a totally different style, I would never make my fortune as a writer. She says she has found the social standing of her sex a dreadful drawback.

MRS. MOREEN Really.

JAMES She loves the story of Madame George Sand, and believes that if she could have had the courage to wear trousers as that lady did, she could have written as well as she.

MRS. MOREEN	Well, at least her son has that qualification. And seems determined to exploit it by having ever so many a pair.
AMY	I did look at one or two of her books, when I was younger, and they seemed to be like...fairy stories, a dreamland where no one ever grows old, or troubled.
MRS. MOREEN	That must be reassuring.
JAMES	Perhaps. I, on the other hand, try — in my clumsy way — to be in some direct relation to life.
MRS. MOREEN	Ah, yes. Life.
	Pause. MRS. MOREEN *is suddenly tired.*
JAMES	Neither has she any appreciation of form. No appreciation of the grand licking into shape a work of art requires. I thought at our discussion this afternoon on that topic you had some very interesting observations.
MRS. MOREEN	Thank you.
JAMES	(*to* AMY) I have always appreciated your mother's little translations, and I suspected she had far and beyond the requisite talents to undertake some serious literary contribution —
AMY	(*tinge of jealousy*) Well, mother...
JAMES	And our discussion has convinced me of it. You should press her on it Amy.

MRS. MOREEN	I have thought about it...but the time. There are quite consuming responsibilities, the children. With a family one has to...look out...(*pause, reviving*) But with such talented children...
JAMES	I'm sure, I'm sure. And you Mr. Pemberton, how are you enjoying your sojourn as tutor with the unpredictable Moreens?
PEMBERTON	It has been...very educational.
JAMES	Do you think such a family might provoke your own literary aspirations?
PEMBERTON	(*hesitant*) Well, I make the occasional contribution to magazines.
MRS. MOREEN	(*genuinely surprised*) Well..!
JAMES	Then you must make the most of such a stimulating environment.

Brief pause.

JAMES	Having fulfilled my social obligations in delivering your daughter, Mrs. Moreen, I should be on my way.
MRS. MOREEN	I was about to serve tea (*indicating tea things*). We won't wait for Mr. Moreen who's looking into some urgent business. (*rising*) Mr. Pemberton is in the middle of helping Morgan grapple with a mathematical problem.
MRS. MOREEN	(*continued, to* PEMBERTON) Perhaps you'd prefer to take your tea with Morgan.
MORGAN	(*appearing at the door, to* PEMBERTON) I think I've almost done it!

JAMES   And this must be the remarkable Morgan.
        Mathematics, eh? How very impressive.

MRS. MOREEN Come and be introduced Morgan.

         MORGAN *reluctantly enters.*

AMY   Morgan. This is Mr. James. Mr. James, this is
        Morgan.

         JAMES *and* MORGAN *shake hands.*

JAMES   I've heard a great deal about you Morgan, and
        have formed a high opinion. It seems you are
        the singular talent of the family.

MORGAN   Then let's hope we can maintain your high
        opinion of me by keeping you ignorant of the
        family.

AMY   Too late, Morgan dear, I think we are quite
        resolved to see more of Mr. James. (*taking*
        JAMES's *arm*)

MRS. MOREEN I think that would be an excellent project for the
        season.

MORGAN   But is Mr. James prepared to be pursued by the
        Moreen's?

         AMY *controls herself.*

JAMES   (*laying his free hand lightly on* AMY's) Perhaps
        an interest in my own education would lead me
        to pursue the Moreens.

MRS. MOREEN Then it's decided Mr. James. We shall be seeing
        more of you.

JAMES   (*hesitating*) Not, I'm afraid, in the immediate future. I've decided to spend the next few months in Paris. I've even obtained a box at the *Comédie-Française*. So I will be leaving in a few days.

MRS. MOREEN   Ah! What a shame.

               MRS. MOREEN *and* AMY *struggle to conceal their disappointment.*

JAMES   But while I must interrupt my education, I trust Morgan will continue to pursue his (*directly to* MORGAN), so he might impress me even more on our next encounter.

MORGAN   Mr. Pemberton is teaching me geometry.

               PEMBERTON *goes to speak.*

JAMES   That is impressive. I always found geometry a very mysterious subject.

MORGAN   That's one of its great advantages. People can know nothing about it and still be impressed.

PEMBERTON   Geometry provides a grounding...it's a good discipline, for study in general, I think. Morgan is so good at languages that there is nothing there that provides any difficulty.

JAMES   I'm sure you can help him surmount the difficulties of both geometry and discipline.

PEMBERTON   (*rising*) Perhaps Morgan and I should be getting back to our studies.

MRS. MOREEN   It is rather late Mr. Pemberton. Morgan should be retiring.

MORGAN   Goodnight, Mr. James.

JAMES   *Bon soir*, Morgan...Mr. Pemberton.

           MORGAN *and* PEMBERTON *exit.*

JAMES   A remarkable little chap. (*rising*) And now I must be going.

MRS. MOREEN   But the tea...

JAMES   No. I must be up early. Preparation for the trip to Paris, you understand.

AMY   Didn't you say earlier, mother, that we might be visiting Paris later in the season?

MRS. MOREEN   Well, yes. That would be a good idea. We are determined to spend part of the autumn in some bracing place.

JAMES   Then I will be able to offer you the hospitality of my box at the *Comédie-Française*.

AMY   That would be wonderful! We must go mother.

MRS. MOREEN   Then we will indeed, *chérie*.

JAMES   Excellent.

MRS. MOREEN   And now you must show Mr. James to the door. (*offering her hand to* JAMES)

JAMES   (*kissing* MRS. MOREEN's *hand*) Au revoir, Mrs. Moreen.

> JAMES *and* AMY *exit.* MRS.
> MOREEN *sits down exhausted, closes
> her eyes. Pause. She quietly hums the
> Neapolitan song. Pause.* AMY *re-enters.
> Pause.*

AMY Did you have to sing that song today?

MRS. MOREEN (*eyes still closed*) Amy, dear, no one there
understood Neapolitan — they didn't understand
the words.

AMY I'm sure Mr. James understood.

MRS. MOREEN No dear. He just likes one to think that he does.

> *The lights go down on* AMY *and* MRS.
> MOREEN.

***

Act One, Scene Seven

Early morning light comes up. Perhaps
PEMBERTON *is asleep.* MORGAN's
bed is unmade. MORGAN *has a bucket
of sand. He very carefully and quietly
begins to pour the sand in lines on the
floor to form a large geometrical shape.*
PEMBERTON *wakes up, or enters.*

PEMBERTON   Morgan? What's going on?

MORGAN   (*quite excited, pointing to the floor*) You see,
here it is.

PEMBERTON   What on earth are you doing?!

MORGAN   (*standing back*) It's the proof.

PEMBERTON   Sand? And that's just a diagram, a single
diagram.

MORGAN   I know, I know!

PEMBERTON   But Morgan, a proof should be more than just a
diagram. You must have understood that at least.

MORGAN   I know. But *look* at it, look at it!

PEMBERTON   (*getting out of bed*) Morgan, please. Calm down.

MORGAN   But look! You can see if you look!

                  PEMBERTON takes MORGAN and
                  sits him down. Pause. MORGAN is
                  breathing hard.

PEMBERTON   Calm down Morgan. Alright. What is this?
                  Explain it to me.

MORGAN   Yes. (*taking a few deep breaths, holding his*
                  chest) Yes. Once you see it, it's obvious, It's
                  completely clear...

PEMBERTON   Calm down Morgan. Now what are you talking
                  about?

MORGAN   Well. (*deep breath, pause*) I'll show you. (*getting*
                  up and walking the shape) See (*pointing*) this is
                  the triangle — the right-angled triangle. Here's
                  the hypotenuse...and that's got to be a square on
                  the hypotenuse. These are the squares on the
                  other two sides...and, together, they've got to
                  equal the first square...

PEMBERTON   But..isn't that just the way you've drawn it?

MORGAN   No. No! That's just it! All you need is the right
                  angle here and it works — whatever the
                  dimensions! (*suddenly gasping for breath*)

PEMBERTON   (*grabbing him*) Morgan.

MORGAN   Geometry's wonderful. It's so clear.

                  PEMBERTON stands and stares at the
                  diagram. Long pause. Music rises over,
                  lights go down slowly.

Act One, Scene Eight

> *A railway platform. The* MOREENS
> *and* PEMBERTON *are crowded together*
> *with various forms of baggage and*
> *trunks. There is a general air of long-*
> *travelled lassitude.* MORGAN *is*
> *sleeping like a child on* MOREEN.

MOREEN The Gare du Nord.

MORGAN (*dreaming, thick sleep-talkers voice*) Are we in Paris?

MRS. MOREEN Yes, my dear.

MOREEN (*to no one in particular*) Cities always appear the same when entered by railway.

MORGAN (*mumbling in his sleep*) Is that what we speak?

MOREEN Approached by steamer on the other hand they always appear quite, quite different.

MORGAN What is it we speak?

MRS. MOREEN *Tu parle très bien le français mon cher. Tu étais à Paris (quand tu étais un jeune garçon).*

MORGAN

(*panic entering his voice*) *Que ça que dicimus...dicere*...say, what do we say...who understands...where —

MRS. MOREEN

Morgan!?

> MORGAN *slowly turns to face her, eyes still glazed.*

MRS. MOREEN

(*softer, reaching out to touch him*) You're dreaming, my love.

MORGAN

(*pushing her hand off, looking dazedly around*) *Quis meum cognoscit?*

MRS. MOREEN

(*over*) *Leibchen...*

MORGAN

Which city? Where are we going?

PEMBERTON

Morgan...

MORGAN

(*turning to* PEMBERTON, *blinking, waking up, voice changing*) Oh. Pemberton. We're here? In Paris?

MRS. MOREEN

(*getting out a thermos flask*) Would you like some tea, Morgan.

MORGAN

I don't drink tea. (*rising*) I'm going for a walk.

> MORGAN *wanders off.*

MRS. MOREEN

Morgan seems a little strained today. Do you think you might be pushing him too hard?

PEMBERTON

Morgan's pushing himself. He even wants to start on the philosophers.

MOREEN

Philosophers did you say, Pemberton?

PEMBERTON	Greek philosophers actually.
MOREEN	Is that a good idea? I would have thought that it might be a little early for that kind of thing, for a young chap...the burden of knowledge, so to speak.
MRS. MOREEN	Why would Morgan be interested in philosophy?
PEMBERTON	I don't know. I mentioned the notion of ethics. He was very intrigued.
AMY	Ethics...?!
PEMBERTON	The study of morals...virtue. Right and wrong.
AMY	Ah, yes. Virtue. You know, I think he was rude with Mr. James. Morgan has been rather funny lately.
MRS. MOREEN	Repartee, dear. Morgan has always been funny.
AMY	I meant funny peculiar, not funny, 'ha, ha'.
MOREEN	(*to* MRS. MOREEN) Have you not felt him to be a little distant, my dear? But then he is of an age...his sap and so forth..
AMY	His sap..?
MOREEN	His...sap.
MRS. MOREEN	Sap, Amy dear, sap.
AMY	Sap.
MOREEN	Must we discuss sap? I hadn't the intention of rendering it the topic of conversation.

MRS. MOREEN   What do you think Mr. Pemberton...on the topic of Morgan and the rising sap.

PEMBERTON   (*embarrassed*) I don't quite see...

MRS. MOREEN   Has it risen...? Because his heart as you know is not strong. And such a rapid broadening of his interests...philosophy, ethics..?

PEMBERTON   He is such an extraordinarily intelligent boy.

        AMY *sighs quietly and looks away.*

PEMBERTON   He's managed to become proficient in Greek in such a short space of time. He even swapped his *Gallic Wars* for a battered copy of one of Plato's dialogues at a Venice bookstore.

MRS. MOREEN   And which dialogue would that be?

        MORGAN *wanders back.*

MOREEN   Mr. Pemberton tells us you have been out getting yourself philosophical texts.

MORGAN   Yes. I got a copy of *The Symposium* in Venice.

MOREEN   Ah, yes. *The Symposium*? That's about ethics, virtue and so forth, isn't it?

MORGAN   No Pater, it's not.

MOREEN   Ah. (*trying to recall*) *The Symposium...The Symposium..?*

        Pause.

MRS. MOREEN   Love. It's about love.

Long silence.

AMY   (*rising*) Where has the bloody porter got to.

End of Act One.

Act Two - Virtue in Paris · Scene One

> *Two months later, late autumn.*
> PEMBERTON *and* MORGAN *are in*
> *The Louvre sitting on a bench staring*
> *out front as if at a painting. It is late*
> *afternoon and throughout the scene the*
> *light is fading.*

PEMBERTON   (*glancing at a catalogue*) And this one?

MORGAN   Clearly a classical theme...

PEMBERTON   Yes...

MORGAN   The...er, nymph is attempting to *filer*..

PEMBERTON   *Filer*..?

MORGAN   In London they'd say 'scapa'. *Fugit.* I think
Americans say 'split'.

PEMBERTON   You mean depart..?

MORGAN   I don't think 'depart' quite captures the sense
of...*presto*.

PEMBERTON   *Presto?* Ah. The situation of the, er, nymph
(*looking at the catalogue*) — Psyche.

MORGAN	With Amor. (*pause*) Perhaps *you* ought to *filer*.
PEMBERTON	(*contrasting Italian & French*) Filer...presto..?
MORGAN	Yes.
PEMBERTON	Apart from recommending a sort of bi-lingual exit, what are you talking about Morgan?
MORGAN	They hardly pay you do they? And you spend what tiny amount of money you have on on books and things for me.
PEMBERTON	(*defensive*) They hardly pay me? What makes you think that?
MORGAN	Because it's true.
PEMBERTON	Not at all.
MORGAN	You really are too good.
PEMBERTON	And what do I want money for..?
MORGAN	Well that is another question!
PEMBERTON	...So you and I can *filer* to some idyllic Aegean isle?
MORGAN	Terrific idea! As soon as you've finished me, we can tutor wealthy youths, and then off to Greece on the proceeds.
PEMBERTON	Meanwhile I shall have to hone my tutoring skills on you.
MORGAN	I suppose that means you want some insightful remarks on the technique, composition, form, on so on, of the *oeuvre*.

MORGAN *and* PEMBERTON *both look out front. Pause.*

PEMBERTON   Careful observation. Insightful, but above all, clear and honest.

MORGAN   (*pause*) Well...I think it's rather interesting that Psyche and Amor have their clothes off.

PEMBERTON   Really, Morgan..

MORGAN   Not clear and honest?

PEMBERTON   Not exactly what I had in mind.

MORGAN   (*looking off*) Look, he's getting up and scratching himself.

PEMBERTON   (*not looking*) If someone is scratching themselves Morgan I'm not sure we should look. At least not both at the same time.

MORGAN   You're right. The way he does it is almost depraved. He always does it just before closing time.

PEMBERTON   Who are you talking about?

MORGAN   The Gendarme, guard, whatever he is. Gets up and scratches himself just before closing time.

PEMBERTON   So you have brought your powers of observation to bear on something.

MORGAN   Can't miss him. Such a funny shape...either his neck's too short or his body's too long.

PEMBERTON   Not only depraved but also deformed...

MORGAN	(*laughing*) I think he's terrific. I love this room, wouldn't mind staying forever, with the classical themes. All these pictures in the Louvre — landscapes and assorted portraits — bishops, knights and soldiers all dressed up, all that other stuff. But as soon as an artist paints something like *Psyche and Amor* all attire is totally abandoned.
PEMBERTON	Not quite totally...
MORGAN	Some well-placed diaphanous drapery.
PEMBERTON	But —
MORGAN	(*interrupting*) And they're beautiful. Why is that? I find them so...beautiful. Even when I know the picture is silly, these bodies seem to mean so much. I can see something like this, or even just think of it, and my mouth goes dry, I can feel my heart. I used to think it was all part of a big joke — that Neapolitan song, the things in the translation. It's like all that stupid business with Amy and which men she should be nice to — the people they're nice to — they just want them to be rich. It's all pretense, a joke. I used to see the paintings, the bodies in the dark churches in Venice. I thought I understood it then, it had nothing to do with me. But now it does. (*pause*) Do you think it's because of my rising sap?
PEMBERTON	I really don't know, Morgan.
MORGAN	I'd never talk to them about it. They'd make fun of me, someway or other. So you'd better say something clear, honest and insightful.
PEMBERTON	(*pause*) I suppose I'm a bit embarrassed.

MORGAN   But you understand don't you?

PEMBERTON   Yes. I understand. I do.

                    Pause.

MORGAN   When I was much younger we would go to the
                    Lido and there would be other children, the
                    urchins from round about — naked — playing in
                    the water.

PEMBERTON   (*pause*) You must have wanted to join them.

MORGAN   Oh, no. No. To have me in amoung them would
                    have spoilt the beauty of it all.

VOICE OFF   *On ferme.*

MORGAN   Time to go, old chap. Time to go.

                    MORGAN *and* PEMBERTON *stand,*
                    the lights fade.

                            ***

Act Two, Scene Two

A short time later, MOREEN *and*
MRS. MOREEN *are sitting down in
the living room.* PEMBERTON *enters.*

MOREEN

Ah, Pemberton my dear fellow, back so soon?
We imagined you to be out with Morgan,
drinking in the great cultural life of Paris.

PEMBERTON

We were out, but Morgan became tired. He's
lying down at the moment.

MRS. MOREEN

Not poorly I hope?

PEMBERTON

No. Simply tired. It is unseasonably cold.

MOREEN

Ah. Well we must be careful Pemberton. Morgan
is not —

PEMBERTON

(*interrupting*) I'm quite aware of Morgan's
condition.

MOREEN

Ah.

MRS. MOREEN

But you understand our concern. (*pause*) How do
you find having a room to yourself?

PEMBERTON

The room is adequate.

MOREEN	These are not of course the rooms we wanted. But unfortunately the apartments we had last time we were in Paris — splendid apartments — are taken. Unfortunately.
PEMBERTON	You had mentioned that.
MRS. MOREEN	I imagine we did.
PEMBERTON	I was rather hoping we might discuss my salary.
MOREEN	Why of course my dear fellow, of course. I take it there might have been an oversight...?
PEMBERTON	Since the beginning of my employment with you in Venice I have received a total of fifteen francs. Although we have still been unable to have any kind of conversation establishing the exact amount of my salary — after several approaches on my behalf I might add — and given that one hundred francs a month is absolutely the least someone in my position should be paid, I shall consider myself forced to leave your employment immediately unless I am paid one hundred francs — immediately.
MOREEN	(*to* MRS. MOREEN) Why an oversight, my dear, a terrible oversight. We are in arrears to Mr. Pemberton. We must settle up without delay. (*to* PEMBERTON) I shall be leaving for London tomorrow morning, Pemberton, and when I return —
PEMBERTON	(*interrupting*) Immediately!
MOREEN	My dear fellow. Please let us be men of the world about —

PEMBERTON   I have no pretensions to being 'a man of the world'...I simply wish to be paid — now. And, once and for all, come to some arrangement.

MRS. MOREEN   This comes as a very sudden and unexpected rebuke from a man who we have trusted with our remarkable child, and whose interest in the well-being of that child we took for granted.

PEMBERTON   Are you going to blackmail me with fears about Morgan — what'll happen to him if I go away..?

MRS. MOREEN   And, pray tell, what *would* happen to him?!

PEMBERTON   He'd be left alone with you!

MRS. MOREEN   And who should he be with but those who cherish him, sacrifice for him, who love him most?

PEMBERTON   So dismiss me! Send me away!

MRS. MOREEN   You think he loves you more than he loves us...than he loves me?!

PEMBERTON   I am the only one I can see making sacrifices.

MRS. MOREEN   (*yelling*) I'm his mother!!!

MOREEN   (*taking hold of* MRS. MOREEN, *sitting her down, calming her*) Please, my dear. Please. Pemberton we must allow ourselves to be practical. We have been ...negligent woefully... But this can be repaired. Indeed. With the family to look out for as my consuming occupation there are oversights. I am clearly in your debt, and as a man of ...(*stalling*) of honour I can assure you that debt will be met with utmost of my ability. It simply requires a small number of

MOREEN (*continued*) days — arranging finances as it were.
It will be foremost in my mind as I sally forth to
London. I will be leaving first thing in the
morning. First thing.

PEMBERTON If we can't settle up within twenty-four hours,
and come to some arrangement, I'll be forced to
leave. (*pause*) And I shall explain to Morgan
exactly why I am leaving.

Pause.

MRS. MOREEN Then the knife is to our throats.

MOREEN You haven't already told him?

PEMBERTON Of course not. What do you take me for?

MRS. MOREEN (*thinking, to herself*) Not enough, it would seem.

Pause.

MOREEN (*quietly*) One hundred francs..? (*to
PEMBERTON*) What use can you have for all
that money, Pemberton, living the quiet life that
we do?

MRS. MOREEN *puts a restraining
hand on* MOREEN's *arm.*

PEMBERTON I will be in my room, packed and ready to leave
by this time tomorrow, unless our accounts are
settled.

MOREEN Pemberton, old chap —

PEMBERTON And I will not be persuaded otherwise! Good
evening.

         PEMBERTON *exits. Pause.* MRS.
         MOREEN *is still thinking.*

MOREEN   Is he pulling our leg, my dear?

MRS. MOREEN   Oh, no. No. He's not 'pulling our leg'. (*pause*)
But perhaps he can be persuaded.

MOREEN   You think so?

MRS. MOREEN   Perhaps. (*pause*) I think you should take the
overnight to London. It leaves in two hours.

MOREEN   You think so my dear?

MRS. MOREEN   Yes, it might be better.

***

Act Two, Scene Three

>*One hour later.* PEMBERTON *is sitting up in bed in his small room, wearing a shirt. There is a quiet double knock at the door.*

PEMBERTON   Yes?

>MRS. MOREEN *enters in a wrap.*

PEMBERTON   (*surprised, pulling a sheet up on himself*) Oh! I thought it would be..

MRS. MOREEN   Mr. Moreen.

MRS. MOREEN   He's left, on the overnight, for London. (*pause*) You see how obliging we are? (*looking around*) But you seem determined to be shot of us.

PEMBERTON   I simply want to be paid.

MRS. MOREEN   'I want to be paid'. Like some petty tradesman. Haven't you learned anything in this time with us — about open-heartedness and sharing?

PEMBERTON   I'm completely broke.

MRS. MOREEN   Here you are in Paris. We brought you here —
the center of the artistic, the civilized world. A
well-appointed hotel. You want for nothing..

PEMBERTON   I had to have my books sold off to pay my debts.

MRS. MOREEN   Do we keep our books with us, dragging them
from city to city?

PEMBERTON   My jacket has just about worn out. I can't even
buy the occasional packet of cigarettes any more.

MRS. MOREEN   (*thrusting a bank note at him*) Here! Here is
money.

PEMBERTON   (*recoiling slightly, brief pause*) Why are you
waving a ten-franc note at me?

MRS. MOREEN   Take it.

PEMBERTON   This is 'open-heartedness'? People spontaneously
shoving banknotes at each other? I have to beg,
to threaten you. Has Mr. Moreen gone to beg
from someone else?

MRS. MOREEN   We are not beggars!

PEMBERTON   He 'sallies forth' — to do what?

MRS. MOREEN   Always the grimy symmetry of the balance
ledger. Why do you colonials always nurture the
meanest aspects of the British character?

PEMBERTON   But I don't understand how you live — how I'm
supposed to live. Moreen has no profession, no
regular income. He disappears for a week or more
and when he returns there might be a sudden
spurt of extravagance, or not. Sometimes you get
a check for translation.

MRS. MOREEN Yes..?

PEMBERTON Amy can have expensive material for frocks —
fresh flowers — while Morgan's clothes are
falling apart, and I am not paid.

MRS. MOREEN My husband, through his services for various
individuals and governments, is able to call on a
number of informal moral obligations from
various wealthy persons. We also have a number
of elderly relatives. Amy has the wardrobe to
match her other...attractions because we
obviously wish to make a good match for her.
Morgan, on the other hand — as you know —,
cares very little about his dress.

PEMBERTON That tells me nothing except that you rely on the
indulgence of old acquaintances and the
generosity of senile relatives to keep you from
poverty.

MRS. MOREEN We're not poor!

PEMBERTON But the chaos, the stupid expenses. Rushing here
to Paris at the drop of a hat...

MRS. MOREEN Amy must marry well! (*biting her tougue, pause*)
We try to be equitable with our children, there are
expenses for Morgan that we did not afford for
Amy...

PEMBERTON ...Like a tutor, you mean..?

MRS. MOREEN Exactly.

> MRS. MOREEN *catches herself, begins
> to laugh.* PEMBERTON *smiles too.
> Pause.*

MRS. MOREEN See! You do enjoy yourself with us. Have you any idea how dull most families are. There are rewards, there are.

PEMBERTON Then perhaps I'm no longer sure if I can afford you.

MRS. MOREEN You mean Morgan.

PEMBERTON What?

MRS. MOREEN If you can afford Morgan.

      Pause. MRS. MOREEN *moves closer to* PEMBERTON.

MRS. MOREEN Can't you understand the rewards of simply being with him, the privilege of knowing and living with him? And the importance of not burdening him with...the awkward things in life.

PEMBERTON (*pause*) You mean I shouldn't tell him I'm paid virtually nothing.

MRS. MOREEN Not unless you want to show off.

PEMBERTON Why me? You're well-read enough to tutor him yourself. You can read Greek, you know the classics.

MRS. MOREEN I don't enjoy the Greeks. And I have neglected the rest of my family. Amy is almost beyond marrigeable age and there are a mother's obligations, and, God knows, that can be a full-time occupation. And my husband deserves a certain amount of attention. He does his best for the family within his limitations.

PEMBERTON Why did you...marry...

MRS. MOREEN Moreen was a very...attractive man, and was one of the indulgences I thought I should allow myself as a passionate young woman. But then I became pregnant with Amy. I haven't always treated him well.

Silence.

PEMBERTON Morgan is an extraordinary boy. I'm fond of him. But right now I can't even afford a haircut.

MRS. MOREEN (*reaching out, touching his head*) I like your hair like this. And if you need, I can cut it.

PEMBERTON ...And then call in the Philistines.

MRS. MOREEN Why don't you write articles, even translate as I do. The family can provide the ideal environment for that.

PEMBERTON Translating pays terribly.

MRS. MOREEN I'm glad to make what I can.

PEMBERTON I'm sorry. I have sent off a few pieces, but they're always refused.

MRS. MOREEN Not such a protégé then, sacrificing your talents for us.

> PEMBERTON *goes to turn away.*
> MRS. MOREEN *grasps his hand with both of hers.*

MRS. MOREEN I'm sorry! You are making sacrifices, you are.

PEMBERTON You're as strange as your son.

MRS. MOREEN   But I understand, I do. (*moving closer*) We all must make sacrifices, but I think they are sacrifices we crave to make.

PEMBERTON   And you?

> MRS. MOREEN *puts* PEMBERTON'*s hand to her breast and holds it there.*

MRS. MOREEN   I too can make sacrifices.

> *Long pause as* MRS. MOREEN *looks at* PEMBERTON.

PEMBERTON   (*with difficulty*) My mouth has gone quite dry.

***

Act Two, Scene Four

> *It is morning of the next day.*
> MORGAN *enters, throws a sheaf of*
> *paper in the air which falls around him.*

MORGAN   You know, I had a dream last night. I was lost in a city. But I think you were there. Do believe in dreams? Not that they predict anything. Just that they mean something. When I was younger, I often had bad dreams, I'd talk in my sleep and so forth...

PEMBERTON   (*entering, fixing his tie*) You still do.

MORGAN   ...If I woke, then Zenobie would come and talk to me about them. She said they always meant something.

PEMBERTON   Who's Zenobie?

MORGAN   She was my nurse, a long time ago. (*pause*) That's how I know they don't pay you.

PEMBERTON   Dream interpretation? That's a little flimsy, isn't it Morgan?

MORGAN   No. I meant Zenobie—

PEMBERTON   — Zenobie's dream interpretation.

>MORGAN *and* PEMBERTON *start to have fun.*

MORGAN   I can assure you, I have more scientific grounds than dream interpretation.

PEMBERTON   Reading tea-leaves perhaps?

MORGAN   (*laughing*) Tea-leaves..?!

PEMBERTON   It's the genteel English form of necromancy. The Chelsea alternative to ripping out the entrails of a cock...or dream interpretation.

MORGAN   Entrails of a cock..?!

PEMBERTON   The Romans. Used to read their stars in chicken giblets...

MORGAN   God! Trust that lot. Any excuse for a disembowelment.

PEMBERTON   ...while the British prefer tea-leaves.

MORGAN   Any excuse to drink tea. Not so hard on the table cloth either I should think.

PEMBERTON   Probably not.

MORGAN   That does seem to be the principal issue for the English.

PEMBERTON   What's that?

MORGAN   Minimum wear and staining of the household linen.

PEMBERTON   Very perceptive, Morgan.

MORGAN	But I imagine tea-leaves make a bit of a mess.
PEMBERTON	They don't chuck them on the table cloth.
MORGAN	They don't?
PEMBERTON	They leave them in the cup.
MORGAN	We should try it some time then.
PEMBERTON	Good idea! What shall we try and predict?
MORGAN	Whether my father's going to pay you anything when he gets back from London.
PEMBERTON	Ah. But you don't drink tea.
MORGAN	You're right.
PEMBERTON	And I'm not English.
MORGAN	Neither am I really. I never lived there...I suppose it'll have to be entrails...

Brief pause.

PEMBERTON & MORGAN	(*together*) No.
PEMBERTON	(*pause*) It seems a rather long time since the Moreens had tea.
MORGAN	That's a relief. It means we don't have those awful people over.
PEMBERTON	Morgan. It's very important for them to take Amy out into good society. It's their duty as parents.

MORGAN	Being so amusing and entertaining to people they sneer at as soon as their backs are turned — who probably sneer at us too because we're poor and scrambling?
PEMBERTON	(*slight hesitation*) You're not *poor*.
MORGAN	Who knows? Weeks of macaroni and coffee. And then off to some 'bracing place' with first-class tickets. I don't understand anymore. I mean, what are they living on? I think the whole thing's going to come to pieces.
PEMBERTON	Is that a prediction?
MORGAN	Yes, it's a prediction.
PEMBERTON	Good thing I'm not superstitious. (*pause*) They are charming, talented...resourceful people though.
MORGAN	Exactly. So why do they have to be such sychophants. Witty and charming to dolts, chasing off to Paris...
PEMBERTON	I don't think it's quite that simple. Anyway James is hardly a dolt.
MORGAN	I don't like him much. You're the only nice person we know, and look how they treat you.
PEMBERTON	They don't treat me badly.
MORGAN	They don't pay you. And I've always known they don't because they didn't pay Zenobie.
PEMBERTON	Ah, yes. Zenobie.

MORGAN   They took you both on knowing they weren't
              going to pay you and hoping you'd stay on
              because we're so *à la mode*.

              MORGAN *is a bit upset. Pause.*
              PEMBERTON *puts his arm around*
              MORGAN's *shoulders.*

PEMBERTON   (*quietly*) Well Morgan. Once encountered it is
              hard to forgo the pleasure of your company.

              Pause.

MORGAN   You have to look for another job, something that
              pays. I'll be alright, I'm almost grown. And then
              we can meet up later, you know. Or maybe we'll
              finish me sooner than you think.

PEMBERTON   (*straightening the books in front of* MORGAN)
              Then I think we'd better get on with it.

MORGAN   Actually, I'm going to lie down. I'm feeling a bit
              tired out. But we're going to write a letter, first
              thing tomorrow. You have friends in London.
              There must be lots of chances for tutors.

              MORGAN *gets up slowly.*

PEMBERTON   (*hesitation*) What is exactly wrong with your
              heart Morgan?

MORGAN   It's called a hole in the heart. I was born with a
              flaw...the blood doesn't flow properly. I'm not
              supposed to exert myself, get excited — I've got
              used to that. But, you know, when people say
              'heart' it seems to mean all kinds of things.

PEMBERTON   That's just superstition.

MORGAN	But I used to wonder. Everyone uses the word flaw...you wonder how flawed you are.
PEMBERTON	I think you're fine, Morgan.
MORGAN	I know.

***

Act Two, Scene Five

> *It is late.* MRS. MOREEN *is in the living room.* PEMBERTON *enters and slowly approaches* MRS. MOREEN.

PEMBERTON   (*quietly*) They're in bed. Morgan's reading. I think Amy's asleep.

MRS. MOREEN   He's still reading.

PEMBERTON   Yes.

> *Pause.*

MRS. MOREEN   I asked him if he'd help me with some translation earlier. He said he was too busy studying. I didn't think to ask him what was so preoccupying.

PEMBERTON   He just started *The Symposium.*

MRS. MOREEN   Ah, yes. *The Symposium.*

PEMBERTON   You've read it?

MRS. MOREEN   Yes.

PEMBERTON   You said you didn't enjoy the Greeks.

MRS. MOREEN   I was thinking of those gorey plays — Oedipus, Medea, and so on.

PEMBERTON   Too epic for your taste?

MRS. MOREEN   Rather too accurately domestic, actually.

> PEMBERTON *quietly laughs.*

MRS. MOREEN   One day you may understand that incest and infanticide are the very stuff of domesticity. We modern people just practice them in a more...intimate garb.

PEMBERTON   Morgan is very taken with the Greeks.

MRS. MOREEN   He seems very preoccupied.

PEMBERTON   Oh he is. Completely absorbed.

MRS. MOREEN   (*carefully*) I still think that a classical education might be pushing him too far.

PEMBERTON   How do you mean?

MRS. MOREEN   It tries to dissect the world so...ruthlessly...

PEMBERTON   Yes..?

MRS. MOREEN   ...I think men, boys, when they have to deal with the passions, like to grasp at simplistic dichotomies...virtue and vice...true and false...men and women...

PEMBERTON   Isn't that just the way things are?

MRS. MOREEN   Not really. How else could you and I be here — like this. (*pause*) It worries me that Morgan may be...hardening, in his attitudes. To things.

Pause.

PEMBERTON   It's difficult to hide my lack of money from him. That you don't pay me.

MRS. MOREEN   You haven't told him, have you?

PEMBERTON   No, I haven't. But he's very perceptive, I'd hate to lie to him about anything.

MRS. MOREEN   You don't have to lie. Just be...ambiguous.

PEMBERTON   And I'm not sure I'd like being 'ambiguous'. Sounds very compromising.

MRS. MOREEN   We are all compromised.

PEMBERTON   I don't think I am.

MRS. MOREEN   Well. Do you want to take Morgan away, to some Greek isle perhaps?

PEMBERTON   Why do you ask that?

MRS. MOREEN   Morgan thinks you do. I think that's because he has some kind of dream...romance...about it, and occasionally you talk about it together.

PEMBERTON   How do you know that?

MRS. MOREEN   We do talk sometimes, me and my son. (*pause*) But I suspect it's not something you'd actually consider, you just don't want to deny him his fancy.

Pause.

MRS. MOREEN   Who knows, when Moreen returns maybe you'll have a salary. Then you won't have to lie to Morgan any more, not about that at least.

PEMBERTON   When is he due back?

MRS. MOREEN   I'm not sure. In about a week, perhaps.

Pause.

PEMBERTON   (*with difficulty*) Can we still be lovers? When he gets back.

MRS. MOREEN *slowly puts her arms around* PEMBERTON'*s neck and kisses him.*

MRS. MOREEN   Wait a little while, till you're sure the children are asleep, and then come to bed.

MRS. MOREEN *exits. Pause while* PEMBERTON *looks after her, then around the room.*

***

Act Two, Scene Six

MORGAN *is standing near center stage, his eyes closed as if in concentration. In the following, though it may not be immediately evident, he is addressing* PEMBERTON *who is off making some coffee.*

MORGAN   (*loudly*) Alright. Pre-Cambrian. Pretty boring, uni-cellular organisms, maybe a few multi-cellular ones. Then, Cambrian and we can get all enthusiasic about trilobites flopping about in warm oceans. Then: Devonian, Silurian, non-vertebrate fish and (*dramatic*) arachnids. Shuffle along to the Carboniferous...so-called by virtue of lush vegetation destined to become coal. Amphibians, preceded by lung-fish I suppose. Then it gets really interesting. Jurassic, Triassic and...

MRS. MOREEN *enters, followed by* AMY.

MORGAN   ...reptiles! Which brings us to those celebrated denizens of the paleolithic world — the (*suddenly seeing* MRS. MOREEN *and* AMY, *his voice drops to a surprised whisper*) dinosaurs...

> *Pause.* AMY *slumps into an armchair while* MRS. MOREEN *starts to remove her gloves.*

PEMBERTON   (*off*) Well..? The what?

MRS. MOREEN   Dinosaurs!

> *Pause.* PEMBERTON's *flustered head appears.*

MRS. MOREEN   A large but extinct reptile, I believe.

PEMBERTON   You're back.

MRS. MOREEN   The morning's duties done. At home with the Dorringtons.

PEMBERTON   I'm making coffee. Would you like some?

MRS. MOREEN   No thank you.

> PEMBERTON *disappears. Pause. He reappears.*

PEMBERTON   Amy?

AMY   No.

> PEMBERTON *disappears.*

MRS. MOREEN   Don't stop on our account, Morgan dear. That looked quite fun.

MORGAN   How was it — The Dorrington's?

AMY   Dull.

MRS. MOREEN   Duller I should imagine than here. Though we did our best to be amusing.

MORGAN   Were they appreciative of the amusing Moreens?

MRS. MOREEN   I think so.

AMY   Lord Dorrington wanted mother to sing. The Neapolitan song.

MRS. MOREEN   He was pining for the 'passionate city of Venice'...waxed poetic on some obscure architectural details.

AMY   ...shed a few tears...

MRS. MOREEN   ...over what turned out to be a rather confused description of Florence..

AMY   ...'Ah, Venezia, Venezia, Venezia!', he said.

MRS. MOREEN   And then — a perfectly appropriate request for a song he couldn't understand, as nostalgia for a city he didn't remember.

AMY   (*singing the first line of the song*)

MORGAN   You were kind enough to oblige him.

MRS. MOREEN   Yes, we were *carissimo*. We should let people have their fancies. Let him put the Vatican in Piccadilly Circus if he likes, and weep over that. (*pause, a hand on* MORGAN) You used to like that song, *liebchen*.

MORGAN *shrugs. Pause.*

MRS. MOREEN I think he was really pining for his plain but passionate Italian mistress, but he couldn't wax poetic on her in front of everybody.

AMY Men are funny. No accounting for their —

MORGAN (*interrupting*) — Sap?

MRS. MOREEN I think Amy was going to say 'taste', dear.

AMY Perhaps it was his sap. He did seem to love her, his passionate Italian mistress.

MORGAN Perhaps he loved her because she was passionate.

MRS. MOREEN Perhaps he did, my love. Perhaps he did. (*pause*) Where has your Mr. Pemberton got to *cher*?

MORGAN *My* Mr. Pemberton, Mater? He must be still making the coffee.

MRS. MOREEN Yes. How nice of him. (*to* AMY) We should freshen up dear. We have two hours before we're due at the Van Houten's, so I thought we might take in something of the Louvre on the way. (*to* MORGAN) You and Pemberton have explored the Louvre, Morgan. Have you a gallery or painting, perhaps, to recommend?

MORGAN (*hesitating*) No, not really.

MRS. MOREEN *exits.*

MORGAN Was James at the Dorrington's?

AMY No, he bloody wasn't. He doesn't seem to be anywhere.

MORGAN   So I suppose you have to go off and be nubile at
                the Van Houten's.

AMY   I'm sick of it. I wish we were rich...rich
                Americans. Then it really wouldn't matter who I
                married.

MORGAN   I don't think it would make any difference now.

AMY   How could you say that?

MORGAN   I don't know. I don't understand the Moreens any
                more. We're not amusing, and it wouldn't make
                any difference if we were rich.

AMY   James might be at the Van Houten's...

MORGAN   But d'you think it can go on like this?

                        PEMBERTON *enters carrying two cups*
                        of coffee.

PEMBERTON   Here's your coffee Morgan. How are you today
                Amy? I'm afraid this is the last of the coffee.

AMY   It's alright. We just had some at the
                Dorrington's. And now we're off to have some
                more at the Van Houten's. And on the way we're
                going to the Louvre.

PEMBERTON   Quite a round of visits.

AMY   I think we're supposed to go to the Louvre before
                luncheon so we miss the hotel manager
                downstairs. He's being very silly lately — keeps
                wanting to talk to father.

                        MRS. MOREEN *enters.*

MRS. MOREEN   Ah. There you are Mr. Pemberton. Amy, we should be going soon, you must get ready dear. (*to* MORGAN) *Liebchen* , I seem to have left my fan *quelque part*. Would you like to look for it?

MORGAN *and* AMY *exit.*

PEMBERTON   You're off to the Louvre?

MRS. MOREEN   Would you like to come? A family outing.

PEMBERTON   I don't think Morgan will. He'll probably want to press on. (*pause*) He's very keen right now. A new topic.

MRS. MOREEN   What topic would that be?

PEMBERTON   An analogy between geometry and ethics.

MRS. MOREEN   I really don't see why you have to indulge in this metaphysical *obscurandus.*

PEMBERTON   Morgan's very curious...

MRS. MOREEN   There's any number of things a boy of his age can be curious about...dinosaurs, tadpoles.

PEMBERTON   And it's not obscure. We are talking about the origins of rational thought, the first formulation of Plato's theory of forms.

MRS. MOREEN   Can you hear how damn pompous you sound?

PEMBERTON   I don't understand. Why are you so upset by this?

MRS. MOREEN   I don't want to be part of a world arbitrated by stupid, smug men acting 'rationally'. I couldn't survive in it. And neither could Morgan.

PEMBERTON This is silly. Out of all proportion. I'm simply
going to teach Morgan...

MRS. MOREEN What, what are you going to teach him? (*pause*)
Well..?

PEMBERTON That ethics can be a system of knowledge like
geometry. Morality can work the same way.
Once you understand the basic axioms — about
virtue, right and wrong — you can work out
exactly how to act, the right thing to do.

MRS. MOREEN You actually believe that?

PEMBERTON Yes. Why not? It's quite straightforward.

MRS. MOREEN I've had a letter from Moreen. He'll be back in
two days. (*pause*) And you received a telegram as
we came in (*producing an envelope and holding it
out*) from England I believe. So straightforward,
isn't it...Life.

> *Pause.* PEMBERTON *takes it and
> moves away to open and read it. He lays
> the envelope on table top.*

MRS. MOREEN I thoughtlessly sent the telegram boy away. I
hope there's no reply.

> *Pause, as* PEMBERTON *reads.*

PEMBERTON A friend has found me a post in London.

MRS. MOREEN Ah. (*pause*) You won't accept it, of course.

PEMBERTON Why shouldn't I? I would finally earn some
money.

MRS. MOREEN What about those magazine pieces you publish?

PEMBERTON   They don't pay me for those...

MRS. MOREEN   If you're so foolish as to work for nothing —

PEMBERTON   You of all people ought to know that!

MRS. MOREEN   Are we nothing?! Is that how we count — for
                   nothing? What about Morgan — finishing his
                   education. Does that count for nothing!?

PEMBERTON   Why is this my responsibility?

MRS. MOREEN   Morgan is the glimmering that something,
                   something in all this, can be different from an
                   endless round of futile vanities. That has been the
                   single sustaining hope. There is nothing else.
                   You see, you have to stay. You can't leave. I
                   won't let you.

                           MORGAN *enters.*

MORGAN   Predictably enough, no fan, *Mater*.

MRS. MOREEN   Would you like to come to the Louvre, Morgan
                   dear?

MORGAN   (*seeing the telegram envelope, picking it up*)
                   What's this? You got a telegram. (*pause*) From
                   London.

                           PEMBERTON *looks at the telegram in
                           his hands. Pause.*

PEMBERTON   It's about a great aunt of mine. She died.

MRS. MOREEN   Poor Mr. Pemberton. You must be kind to him
                   today *carissimo*. Well, Amy and I must be gone
                   to the Louvre.

MRS. MOREEN *exits. Pause.*
PEMBERTON *is distracted.*

MORGAN   So did you inherit tons of money? Set us up for life?

PEMBERTON   What? No.

MORGAN   Doesn't matter. I'll be old enough to make money soon. Finish my education and we can go where ever we like.

***

Act Two, Scene Seven

> MRS. MOREEN *and* PEMBERTON
> *are in* PEMBERTON's *bed looking*
> *languidly 'apres-sex.'.* MRS. MOREEN
> *is, lying on her front,* PEMBERTON *is*
> *sitting up alongside her, stroking her*
> *naked back. Pause*

MRS. MOREEN   I think we're going to the *Comédie-Française*
tomorrow, when Moreen gets back. Would you
like to come?

PEMBERTON   How can we afford the *Comédie-Française?*

MRS. MOREEN   We are invited by Mr. James to share his box.
He made a point of inviting the whole family.

PEMBERTON   I'm not the family.

MRS. MOREEN   Morgan wouldn't go without you.

PEMBERTON   You spoke to him?

MRS. MOREEN   Yes. I spoke to him.

> *Pause.*

PEMBERTON   I didn't realise that you had seen James again. I got the impression he was rather hard to pin down.

MRS. MOREEN   Quite a social whirl.

PEMBERTON   Wouldn't it be better if just Amy went, with a chaperon?

MRS. MOREEN   Now, Mr. Pemberton, aren't you being a little calculating? Anyway, patronising the entire family will titilate his feelings of magnanimity.

PEMBERTON   Wouldn't it be better to count on Amy's powers of seduction.

MRS. MOREEN   Careful. That is my daughter of whom you speak.

PEMBERTON   She is a very charming young woman. She can charm James.

MRS. MOREEN   I'm beginning to think that Mr. James is not very interested in women.

PEMBERTON   He seemed to flirt with you quite heavily.

MRS. MOREEN   He finds me entertaining, just as I find him entertaining. He flirts with me because he knows nothing will come of it.

PEMBERTON   Nothing would come of it?

MRS. MOREEN   How could it? I'm a married woman with a family.

Pause.

MRS. MOREEN   In your case I'm...looking out.

PEMBERTON   'Looking out'..?

MRS. MOREEN   For the family. For Morgan.

PEMBERTON   How reassuring.

MRS. MOREEN   Oh, come on. You mustn't allow your male vanity to confuse a perfectly comfortable arrangement. You will be staying with us for a while longer, which is admirable — for Morgan's sake. And quite pleasant for us — for we two.

PEMBERTON   I hoped there might be some true intimacy, being here, like this...We could allow ourselves some genuine affection.

MRS. MOREEN   Of course. (*kissing him gently*) Nothing but truely intimate. Which is why being here, like this *carissimo*, we shouldn't be hypocrites.

PEMBERTON   To put that in plain, unambiguous language you're telling me you like me just enough for this, so you can keep me around for Morgan's sake.

MRS. MOREEN   Yes. I think I might be telling you that. Does that upset you?

PEMBERTON   No. That doesn't upset me, not that itself, in particular. What upsets me is that you are so busy practicing your repartee, so you can ingratiate yourself with James and the rest of them, that you don't ever get around to any real feelings or passion about anything.

MRS. MOREEN   (*pause*) You mean you.

PEMBERTON   What?

MRS. MOREEN	You mean passion about you. I can't help but feel that's a somewhat self-interested suggestion.
PEMBERTON	No. No. Do it for yourself! Let go. What would it take for you to turn round and tell James and all the rest of those snobs to go to hell. Just like that, 'Go to hell!'.
MRS. MOREEN	Have you any idea how sick I am of being gay. How exausting it is to be interesting, entertaining? But we cannot afford not to be.
PEMBERTON	What is it you can't afford? Because it sounds like your 'not affording' involves sleeping with me while making damn sure you don't become in any way attached.
MRS. MOREEN	Not uncommonly a woman's lot.
PEMBERTON	Like those women walking the streets down by Les Halles, you mean?

> MRS. MOREEN *slaps* PEMBERTON *hard across the face.*

MRS. MOREEN	Yes like them. Except I'm only humiliated by one stupid boy, while they have to put up with a whole stream of them.

> MRS. MOREEN *is up, rapidly dressing herself.* PEMBERTON *grabs her wrist from the bed.*

PEMBERTON	Stay. Stay with me now. Stay else I'll leave. I'll leave and I won't come back. Stay for Morgan's sake.

> MRS. MOREEN *stops and sits on the bed. Pause. Lights down slow.*

Act Two, Scene Eight

> MOREEN *enters looking 'apres-*
> *Comédie-Française', smoking a cigar,*
> *and a little drunk.* PEMBERTON *enters.*
> *Pause.*

PEMBERTON   Was your trip to London successful?

MOREEN   Damn fine gesture of James — inviting us to his box, don't you think Pemberton?

PEMBERTON   I was rather expecting he'd be there.

MOREEN   Busy man — commitments. Called away no doubt, things to look out for. No doubt deeply apologetic and so forth. And two bottles of champagne. Unequalled hospitality. He must be quite taken, with at least one member of the family. Don't you think dear? Dear?

> MRS. MOREEN *enters, deep in*
> *thought, holding, and looking at the*
> *cards attached to, two very elegant*
> *bunches of flowers.*

MRS. MOREEN Mr. James' magnanimity this evening is boundless. He sent flowers.(*holding out a bunch to* PEMBERTON)

MRS. MOREEN   Mr. Pemberton. (*pause*) These are for you.

PEMBERTON   For me..?!

MRS. MOREEN   For you.

PEMBERTON   (*still not taking them*) He sent flowers for me?

MOREEN   For Pemberton..?

MRS. MOREEN   (*holding out flowers to* MOREEN) And for you too, my dear.

> *Pause.* PEMBERTON *and* MOREEN *stare at the flowers.*

MRS. MOREEN   Well take the bloody things.

> MRS. MOREEN *throws the flowers at* PEMBERTON *and* MOREEN *who, awkwardly, catch them.* MRS. MOREEN *exits only to return with three more bunches of flowers.*

MRS. MOREEN   They were delivered while we were at *La Comédie*.

> MRS. MOREEN *tosses two of the bunches onto the sofa and sits down to open an envelope.*

MRS. MOREEN   (*waving the envelope*) The apology no doubt, it has about it a cold, dismissive air. Really Mr. Pemberton, no reason to feel embarrassed. Each member of the household received a wreath. No doubt the maid would have got a posy, if James could just have known her name. Imagine it's from your lover. (*reading the note, pausing as it is quite long*) This man obviously understands

MRS. MOREEN   (*continued*) the grand licking into shape a
                communication of this kind requires...(*still
                reading*) gratitude for attentions paid...exquisite
                remorse for opportunities lost...vague hopes for
                the future, tempered by despair at the
                impossibilities of the present...a parenthetical
                mention of Amy (*looking up*) as a sensitive
                acknowledgement of our intentions (*back to
                letter*)...quasi-philosophical ruminations on fate,
                chance and what-might-have-been...rounded off
                with deeply solicitous aspirations for our present
                and future well-being.

                        Silence.

MOREEN   Will he be calling on Amelia?

MRS. MOREEN   No, dear. He will not be calling on Amelia. Mr.
                James will not be doing that. After a hectic
                sojourn in Paris, Mr. James finds the need to
                return to his native New York.

MOREEN   New York. (*pause*) Is there anything to be done?

MRS. MOREEN   No. There is nothing. Nothing to be done.
                Nothing to be done at all. I have called. I have
                left notes. I have promenaded with Amy in the
                correct *environs*. I have taken her to the right
                *soirée*s. I have charmed and gossiped with the
                right people. I have smiled till my cheeks were
                sore, and coined stupid witticisms till my brain
                ached. But this letter makes it clear that, in the
                case of Mr. James, there is nothing to be done.

MOREEN   Nothing? Nothing to be done?

MRS. MOREEN   Nothing. Let's not try and look too ridiculous in
                front of the help, dear.

> MRS. MOREEN *begins to tear up the letter very slowly and deliberately. Voices of* MORGAN *and* AMY - *off.* MORGAN *enters, looking exhausted, and* AMY, *looking angry.*

AMY   Fucking stupid farce.

> MOREEN *reacts, chokes on cigar.*

MRS. MOREEN   Come over here Morgan, darling.

> MORGAN *goes over to* MRS. MOREEN *who sits him next to her, puts her arms round him and holds him tenderly*

MOREEN   I don't understand —

MRS. MOREEN   (*interrupting*) — And we graciously accept the limits of your understanding. (*to* AMY) What fucking farce were you referring to, dear? The One-Act at the theatre or the serial with James?

AMY   (*collapsing in tears next to* MRS. MOREEN) Oh, God, Mother. It's so humiliating.

MRS. MOREEN   (*arm around* AMY) I know dear. I know. I know.

> MORGAN *has discovered two bunches of flowers by almost sitting on them. He unostentatiously examines them and the notes attached.*

MORGAN   (*rising*) I think I'm going to bed.

MRS. MOREEN   Are you alright dear?

MORGAN   I'm fine. Just tired. It's Amy that's suffering.

MORGAN *exits.*

AMY
I have a headache from that stupid play.

MRS. MOREEN
Perhaps you should lie down.

AMY
I think I will.

AMY *rises. Pause.*

MOREEN
I hope the play was not too crude for Morgan, too risqué. (*to* PEMBERTON) His sap you know.

AMY
What about *my* sap! Why are we always talking about Morgan's sap!

MOREEN
He's not strong dear. His heart.

AMY
I'm not strong! What about my heart! I'm nearly twenty four, I haven't got a husband, I haven't got a lover. Some women have both. I haven't got anything.

MOREEN
We want you to marry well.

AMY
If I marry rich that doesn't mean you'll automatically have money. You'll have to ask us, ask *me*. Are you ready for that — ?

MRS. MOREEN
(*quietly*) Oh, yes.

AMY
— being humiliated the way I have?

AMY *goes to leave.*

MOREEN
But. Amy. Mr. James sent flowers.

AMY *stops. Pause. Rallentando.*

AMY	(*quiet, unsure*) What?
MRS. MOREEN	(*carefully, tenderly*) I can put them in your room, Amy dear.
AMY	Flowers..?

Pause.

MRS. MOREEN	(*rising, holding out a bunch of flowers to* AMY) Mr. James sent these flowers for you.

Pause. AMY *is focused entirely on the flowers in* MRS. MOREEN *arms. She takes them tentatively.*

AMY	(*quiet*) Was there a note?
MRS. MOREEN	There's a card — here.
AMY	(*reading the card*) 'For Amy'.

Pause.

MRS. MOREEN	Perhaps you should lie down now, Amy.
AMY	Yes.

AMY *turns to leave,* MRS. MOREEN *follows her closely. As* AMY *glances at* PEMBERTON, *she notices the flowers hanging down from his hand by his side. She stops.*

AMY	Flowers..?
PEMBERTON	I'm sorry?
AMY	You have some flowers, too.

PEMBERTON   Yes. Yes I do.

AMY   (*taking in the room for the first time*) There seems to be a lot of flowers.

> *Silence.*

MOREEN   Mr. James kindly sent flowers for everybody.

AMY   Pemberton?

MRS. MOREEN   And Mr. Pemberton.

AMY   (*quietly*) Ah.

> AMY *looks down at her flowers, pauses, then takes the end of the stems, swings, and smashes the flowers against the door-jam with all her strength, repeatedly. As she loses control, she begins to scream a kind of ugly, pre-linguistic, infantile vowel.*

AMY   Aaaah!

> *Through the flurry of petals,* MOREEN *steps forward as if to intervene.* AMY *attacks him with the flowers and he backs off, hurt.* AMY *staggers through the room lashing out at anything then falls to her knees.* MRS. MOREEN *steps forward and takes* AMY *in an embrace.* AMY *struggles violently for a few moments, then relaxes completely, dropping the smashed flowers, moaning incoherently.*

AMY *exits sobbing, supported by*
MRS. MOREEN. PEMBERTON *sits,*
shocked. Long pause.

MOREEN   I went to London...to look out. My real
occupation...theory of life, so to speak.
We...look out. As frank, earnest people. My
daughter Amelia...does up her hair. My wife is
able to make...decisions, in my absence. For the
character and culture of our own son Morgan. So
I hope we can count on you...in that regard.

Long pause.

***

Act Two, Scene Nine

Impression of a street at evening.
MORGAN *and* PEMBERTON *are*
dawdling. MORGAN *appears fatigued.*

PEMBERTON   I think we should be getting back, Morgan.
(*looking at him*) You should lie down for a
while.

Pause.

MORGAN   It's getting chilly. (*pause*) I don't really want to
go back. (*pause*) We could go off somewhere.

PEMBERTON   Somewhere..?

MORGAN   Yes. Let's go somewhere. Somewhere warm.
Suffused with soft Aegean light. Where nymphs
gambol.

PEMBERTON   It's a bit late for that. And we can always take
another trip to the Louvre tomorrow.

MORGAN   At least it's late enough that we won't have to
have dinner with the rest of the family.

PEMBERTON   Why are you so unkind about the family
Morgan?

MORGAN   I've stopped caring about them.

PEMBERTON   Morgan, Morgan. That's not true. (*pause*) Your mother cares deeply about you.

MORGAN   Does she care about anything else? Does she care about you?

Pause.

PEMBERTON   I don't know.

***

Act Two, Scene Ten

A few minutes later, in the apartments, untidy and chaotic with half-dead flowers strewn about and, open, half-filled suitcases lying on the floor. MRS. MOREEN is sitting in the middle of it all. She seems to have been crying. PEMBERTON and MORGAN enter and take it all in. MORGAN is shaken.

MRS. MOREEN   Things are...a little untidy.

PEMBERTON   They wouldn't serve us dinner downstairs.

MRS. MOREEN   The management is being a little difficult at the moment.

MORGAN picks up some of his books stuffed into a suitcase.

MORGAN   What are these doing here — from my room?

MORGAN exits hurriedly.

MRS. MOREEN   Morgan..! (*to* PEMBERTON) You took him too far.

PEMBERTON   Is that Amy's crying...in her room?

MRS. MOREEN   Poor Amy.

> MORGAN *enters.*

MORGAN   Someone's emptied our rooms! Father's lying on the bed, in his coat.

MRS. MOREEN   He's resting. He's very tired...

MORGAN   From 'looking out', perhaps?!

MRS. MOREEN   Yes. I expect so.

MORGAN   (*excited*) What does that mean?!

MRS. MOREEN   Morgan, darling, you must calm down. Your heart...

MORGAN   My *heart*..?!

PEMBERTON   (*holding* MORGAN) Morgan! Please..

MORGAN   (*to* PEMBERTON) I told you. It's come to pieces. It's all come to pieces!

> MRS. MOREEN *also holds* MORGAN, *who seems to be losing control, and they help him to a chair.*

MRS. MOREEN   *Carissimo*, please. Quietly, quietly.

> *Pause, as they settle* MORGAN *down.*

MRS. MOREEN   (*standing*) As you see, deeply unfortunate circumstances...have fallen. We have to take ourselves in hand, to turn things about.

MRS. MOREEN *speaks directly to* PEMBERTON.

MRS. MOREEN   Obviously this will require a great deal of attention, from both Mr. Moreen and myself, to the proper adjustment of our affairs. Great sacrifices will have to be made. We are prepared for this. The hardest thing will be to be away from our dear Morgan. But knowing he is under your protection, Mr. Pemberton, this is the only way we could possibly reconcile ourselves to the separation.

PEMBERTON *reacts.*

MRS. MOREEN   I know you have only our best interests at heart. And if we, Mr. Moreen and myself, can convince our dear Morgan to go with you, to accomodate himself to depending on you —

PEMBERTON   (*softly*) *What..?!!*

MRS. MOREEN   We trust you. We really feel we can trust you.

PEMBERTON *turns away.*

MRS. MOREEN   It will be hard for us, very hard. But I'm convinced it is for the best. I'm sure it is.

MORGAN   You mean he can take me away?!

MRS. MOREEN   Yes, he can take you away.

MORGAN   And we can go anywhere we want?!

MRS. MOREEN   Yes, anywhere you want to.

MORGAN   (*triumphant*) How about that. We can go!

> PEMBERTON *turns, his face aghast.*

PEMBERTON   But Morgan...!

MORGAN   Pemberton —

> MORGAN *slides from the chair on to the floor.* PEMBERTON *and* MRS. MOREEN *leap forward to catch him and hold him.*

PEMBERTON   Morgan! I didn't —

> MORGAN *is limp.*

MRS. MOREEN   (*screaming*) Morgan!!

***

Act Two, Scene Eleven

Months later, lights up on MRS. MOREEN *sitting, almost as if in a trance, on a Venice beach looking out at the audience. Sand, is slowly spilling out of her hand. It is important that, throughout this scene, she continues to be self-absorbed, hardly aware of* JAMES. *Even her final line is delivered, to herself, as if it were a kind of private joke. Pause,* JAMES *enters.*

JAMES   (*half recognising* MRS. MOREEN) Mrs. Moreen..?

MRS. MOREEN   What? Oh, James. Mr. James. In Venice.

                          Pause.

JAMES   Do I detect a reproach for my desertion in Paris.

MRS. MOREEN   What? Oh no. No.

                          Pause.

JAMES   How is Mr. Moreen...the family?

MRS. MOREEN   Mr. Moreen is away.

JAMES   Away..?

MRS. MOREEN   Trying to raise money.

JAMES   I see. (*pause*) And Amelia?

MRS. MOREEN   Amy has married — a prince.

JAMES   My...congratulations.

                    Pause.

MRS. MOREEN   You had no intentions towards Amy, did you?

JAMES   No.

                    Pause.

JAMES   And how is Mr...er...Pemberton, our aspirant
                    writer.

MRS. MOREEN   He's returned to Canada.

JAMES   Not pursuing a literary career then..

MRS. MOREEN   I understand they do have literature in Canada.

JAMES   He must have finished Morgan then.

MRS. MOREEN   Morgan's dead.

JAMES   Dead!?

MRS. MOREEN   Dead. He died.

JAMES   I'm...I had no idea.

MRS. MOREEN   Don't let us talk about it...

JAMES   I should —

MRS. MOREEN   (*interrupting*) It doesn't lend itself to
                     'conversation'.

                              Pause.

JAMES   I have found there is comfort in...

                              MRS. MOREEN *looks at* JAMES *for
                              the first time.*

JAMES   ...in my Art.

MRS. MOREEN   (*looking out again*) In its direct relation to life,
                     you mean?

JAMES   Yes.

MRS. MOREEN   (*smiling to herself*) Go to hell, James. Go to
                     hell.

                              The End.